Hawaii
ALOHA

Printed in the United States of America
First Printing, 2018

Made in the USA
Middletown, DE
19 July 2022

69680874R00064